Copyright © 2025 by David W. Bland

All rights reserved.

No part of this publication may be reproduced, distributed, or transmitted in any form or by any means, including photocopying, recording, or other electronic or mechanical methods, without the prior written permission of the publisher, except as permitted by U.S. copyright law.

ISBN: 979-8-9991603-2-4

THE HOLY BIBLE, NEW INTERNATIONAL VERSION®, NIV® Copyright © 1973, 1978, 1984, 2011 by Biblica, Inc.® Used by permission. All rights reserved worldwide.
The ESV® Bible (The Holy Bible, English Standard Version®), © 2001
Some Scriptures are quoted from the King James Version, KJV

Publisher: Greater Is Required, LLC Publishing Services

ENCOURAGEMENT	6
ACKNOWLEDGEMENT	7
PREFACE	8
INTRODUCTION	9
CHAPTER 1	10
Addiction: The Cycle of Self-Sabotage	10
CHAPTER 2	14
Abuse: Toxic Affection & Unauthorized Access	14
CHAPTER 3	19
Rejection: Feeling Unwanted & Unloved	19
CHAPTER 4	22
Depression: Silent But Deadly	22
CHAPTER 5	25
Identity Crisis: Who Am I?	25
CHAPTER 6	28

Abandonment: Dropped, Damaged, Devastated — 28

CHAPTER 7 — 34

Unforgiveness: The Corrosive Cancerous Cycle — 34

CHAPTER 8 — 38

Betrayal: Charged With Attempted Murder — 38

CHAPTER 9 — 42

Pride: Chest Out, Heart Broken, Chest Out — 42

SCRIPTURES — 47

WHAT ARE YOUR TRIGGERS? — 51

TRIGGERS QUESTIONNAIRE — 53

SWIRL QUIZ: THE FIVE STAGES OF ABANDONMENT — 55

RESOURCES FOR MEN'S WELLBEING — 57

ABOUT THE AUTHOR — 58

Encouragement

My friend, as you read this book, I am certain you will find yourself somewhere in the text, as I did while writing. You will experience some tears, some pain, some places that will be uncovered so you can HEAL. Heal from your trauma, heal from the things that really hurt you, heal from the pain of unanswered questions. There is a Balm in Gilead, healing is available to you.

You will finally be able to address your giant, as David did Goliath in 1 Samuel 17:46, and declare, TODAY that which has been haunting me, disturbing me, and even trying to kill my purpose will no longer have dominion over me. God is with you. You can do it. I'm already proud of the steps you are taking. Go forth and be great. I stand as living a witness, God did it for me and still doing it for me. I believe for you. It's time to heal.

Acknowledgement

First, I want to thank my Lord & Savior Jesus the Christ, who does all things well, and made this possible.

I want to thank my parents, Jimmy and Annie Bland for their wisdom, lessons, love, & support.

To my family who have supported me, you know who you are Thank you!

To my friends near and far who have stuck by me, Thank You! To the best church a Pastor could ever ask for, my Refreshed by Fire Tabernacle church family, Thank You!

Last, but certainly not least, to my lovely lady who has stuck with me through it all, Tina Brantley, THANK YOU!! We are going up from here.

Preface

Loneliness, depression, untold secrets, unhealed areas of life, so many questions as to why? Why did this happen to me? Why do I feel so alone? So many emotions floating to the surface that have been pressed down, looked over, or just plain ignored for sake of masculinity. Wait that's right, I am a man, I'm built tough, I'm supposed to be untouchable, unstoppable, and unbreakable. Yet, I find myself at my breaking point, I feel like I'm having a breakdown, but nobody knows, I feel like nobody understands or cares. My struggles I keep to myself, I don't want to appear weak, or not in control of my life. Truth is, I'm tired, I'm really tired. I need a way out. I need to be rescued.

God, do you see what I'm going through? I need healing. I'm ready to take off this mask and live for real. God I'm ready to have this conversation with you. It's time. I can no longer hide. Emancipate me, free me from myself, my addictions. My hope is in you. This is me. No title, no facade, just me. I'm ready to be free.

Introduction

What makes a man a man? Is it his clothes? Is it his money? Is it biological DNA? Society views, and defines a man in different aspects. Largely, this is due to the content of the culture, or the societal constructs that have been given. It is also due to the norms changing as times have changed. People have now evolved into forward thinking, and certain perspectives (sometimes skewed or selfish). With that being said, there is no definitive way to define, or characterize what a male should be, but there is one thing that remains constant , and consistent all are dealing with things behind closed doors, all have some type of struggle, or obstacle they are facing or have faced, and all whether currently ,or in the future want an end or resolve to the chaos, the secret torment, the stress, and pressures of life. Men are programmed to be strong, fearless, never to show emotions, and never really express feelings in a healthy manner.

We are taught to "man up". So, while this has become normal, a shell is created. A shell represents a hardened outer casing in which the REAL being resides. In other words, what you see on the outside is not what's really on the inside. It is a mask. A created, non-permeable, representation of covered bondage, struggle, and often times silent turmoil that is dressed up in security. Journey with me, as we converse, and reveal what lies behind the mask.

Chapter 1

Addiction: The Cycle of Self-Sabotage

What do you call something that gives you a case of the "can't help it's"? It's something that drives you and motivates you to get it no matter what. This something makes you idolize it, placing you above morals, sober thinking, and even in its worst state, placing it before God, and His principles of the Word. That my friend, is an addiction. It makes you lawless, careless, and fruitless. We define addiction as a chronic condition characterized by compulsive, and persistent engagement in a substance or behavior despite negative consequences, and harm to a person.

You lose control. It is a cycle, a viscous, unrelenting, perpetual cycle that ends in two ways death or destiny. It is both physical, and mental as both are affected when you're seeking to feel good, or get some relief. Addictions don't just start overnight in most cases. You are groomed, seduced, and made comfortable with the very thing that is trying to kill you.

Addiction has no favorites. As everyone, not just you is a

casualty.

Addiction masks itself as innocent curiosity, but behind the curiosity lies a beast and the enemy lurking, waiting. 1 Peter 5:8 tells us, "Be sober, be vigilant; because your adversary the devil, as a roaring lion, walketh about, seeking whom he may devour" Addiction calls you by your name, talking sweetly, luring you to satisfy your deepest desire, your most intense cravings. Most addictions with men are never spoken out loud because it is a secret.

Many men are functioning, yet are dysfunctional. They don't want anybody to know what's going on. One bad reveal could ruin a whole relationship, affect ministry, affect those connected to you, or worse you can end up in a dire situation that can lead to the loss of life. Again, because addiction doesn't care who you are, your demographic, or culture, it wants what it wants.

The reason why addiction can be, or is so dangerous is because when you realize you have one, you have already gone in deep. You have opened the door to demonic oppression, and more often than not don't want deliverance, or freedom from it. This allows more spirits to attach to you. It starts with one, and then it becomes many. Normally spirits come in groups. One is a gateway, then the others follow. An example, or proof of this can be found in Luke chapter 8 around the 26 verse. He begins to tell the story of Jesus coming ashore on His travels, and meeting this demon possessed man. Around verse 28, the Bible records that when he saw Jesus, he began to cry out "what do you want with me, don't torture me." Verse 30 is where Jesus began to pose the question "What is your name"? He replied, "Legion for we are many." You are literally killing yourself, and don't realize it. Why? Because it feels good. You want to chase the next high, you want to see how far you can go.

People become addicted for several reasons: escaping reality, easing the indwelling pain, exposure to outside stimuli, being inappropriately touched, dealing with stress, or even family history. Yes, some men are predisposed to certain addictions. It is a harmful cycle of self-sabotage. It is a downward spiral that you can see, and now you have become one with it. You will do whatever, or whoever to satisfy the insatiable appetite for what feels so good, but yet is causing you to live in a false reality. You are sabotaging everything else in your life that's real.

The greatest of leaders, struggle with some form of addiction. Even in ministry, Pastors struggle with addiction such as alcoholism, perversion, and drug use. It's often done behind closed doors, in secret. Why? Because there's an image to uphold. Another reason is the fear of being exposed to those who look up to them. Many men are in relationships with their spouses, but they are not happy. Having a temporary moment of pleasure seems harmless, but it brings forth a cycle, that will eventually get you caught up. I have a question to ask you. WHAT IS in your life that you can't do without? WHAT IS controlling your mind, and heart in the hours of the night when nobody can see you? WHAT IS the one thing that you know you are doing that you know is unhealthy, and you know God is not pleased with it? It's time you get help before it's too late. Run to Jesus, and ask Him sincerely to take it away. Get therapy and/or counseling. What you value above God He will, if it's not handled, take His hand off of your life. My final question is do you love God more than your addiction?

Chapter 2

Abuse: Toxic Affection & Unauthorized Access

We hear about it all the time, the concept of abuse. We hear it more that women are being abused, and of course we as the men are the aggressors. How often do you hear of a man being abused, and put on display? Truth is a lot of men have faced some form of abuse. It's often too painful to speak on. It's too fresh to want to re-live it. The memories haunt you. You are tortured in your mind. You are numb. How would you define abuse? Some say repetitious acts of physical violence, some would say taking lackluster displays of affection, or even taking repeated losses because you love the individual.

The official definition of abuse is improper, or excessive use or treatment, language that condemns, or vilifies usually unjustly, intemperately, and angrily. It's also defined as physical maltreatment, or deception. As a man, our habits, our assimilations, and our interactions start off in childhood as we are groomed to be productive members of society. We are taught to be strong providers, great husbands, and be leaders.

One would say they possess these traits, but at what cost? Many men have gone through traumatic experiences with people they love, and trusted. Ones they call mom, dad, sister, cousin, brother, uncle etc. These have happened many times behind closed doors. No warning, no symptoms, no signs. Just normal dysfunction that makes you seem alright. You do normal day-to-day activities. Still going, still moving, but yet at a standstill. Time for everyone else is moving rapidly, but for you you're frozen in time. Triggers have become normal for you.

You are screaming on the inside, where nobody can hear you. Many men see the cycle of abuse manifesting, but where does it come from? Many of us can recognize why we act the way we do. Some recognize it, but don't want to address it. We hurt so much inside because of the abuse we took as children. Some parents called it discipline, or tough love. To us, it was more of why would you try to hurt me like that?

So many men walk around as hurt adults because they never healed from childhood. Having words spoken to you that cut you like a knife, from those who are supposed to protect you, really carries long term effects on your emotions, and your mental state. Being told things like, "you're a failure," or "your just like your daddy" causes a man to develop directly, or indirectly negative behaviors. It becomes a seed that is planted, and grows overtime from a small plant to a huge forest. Abuse is often multi-faceted, vertical, and horizontal as it can expand into different directions, and can change forms according to the individual.

Every man is different. One may experience one or several types of abuse. Where do you find yourself? Have you experienced mental abuse? That is where a person plays mind games, tries to exhibit control, and forms of manipulation (which is also witchcraft). You may have experienced verbal abuse. The words that were spoken degraded you in such a way that you felt less than, useless, and dehumanized.

Proverbs 18:21 tells us "Death and life are in the power of the tongue", and to a man harsh words will cause you to want to die inside. This is especially true, because of our natural sense of pride, and our unspoken level of vulnerability. Once we have been mishandled or breached, "holes in the soul" are created. Once that takes place it is hard to snatch one back into reality and trust. It is more shocking during verbal abuse, men are emasculated which leads to experiencing symptoms of an identity crisis. Not only do men experience mental abuse and verbal abuse, but some have had experienced extreme punishment where you were whooped mercilessly. Sometimes for stuff you were accused of doing.

As you have gotten over, you have adopted those same characteristics with your children, and the cycle continues. Your children, and your spouse are suffering from things they are not aware of. You were hurt as a child, and grew into a grown man.

Hurt. Broken. Bitter. you express yourselves through pain, anger, and toxic affection. Again, you call it love, but the ones affected call it unfair. You call it being strong, they call it breaking them down. It's truly something to cause someone innocent, that you are called to carry and protect, so much pain because of what someone did to you or didn't do for you. There is another type of abuse that men don't talk about because it is unmentionable. It's embarrassing, painful, and misunderstood. You fear being judged or looked as less than a man.

It's time to talk about it. Sexual abuse. It has happened to many men more than it is verbalized. The shame, and reminders often plague your mind. You are haunted by the thoughts that someone touched you inappropriately. You may have been molested, or you may have been raped. Many times, it is those in our families that we are close to. For example, your mom leaves you with your cousin that's older than you and he/she took advantage of your body and prompted you not to say a word. Perhaps, a religious leader knew you as a kid from a broken home (dad not present, mom running wild), and decides to take you under his wing. While he took you in, he gained your trust, and then violated you. It's ironic because love was shown but it was toxic.

As much as you sought to be loved, appreciated, wanted, and just to be happy, the approach, and the access was unauthorized. It was not warranted. You were left with scares.

You were scared. You didn't know who to trust. As you tried to cope, you developed a hard shell. You developed a disdain for other men who reminded you of your violator. Not only that, you developed two or more identities within yourself (that's another chapter). One is the protected you, the other is the hidden you. Look deep in yourself, and ask yourself… What do I see when I look in the mirror? Is my life patterned after the turmoil and trauma or do I see myself healed?

Chapter 3

Rejection: Feeling Unwanted & Unloved

Have you ever given yourself to someone, or something, and the act was not reciprocated? How did it make you feel when you tried to adapt, change, or lose yourself in attempts to gain love, and acceptance. You, my friend, have experienced rejection. It is a by product of inward trauma that is hidden. It is like a chameleon, as it cloaks itself, and changes forms. Through the spirit of offense, it manifests to cause harm directly or indirectly, intentionally or unintentionally. In either case, it hurts. It is painful. It produces after its own kind.

To better understand rejection, we must define it. It is defined as intentionally or unintentionally excluding, dismissing, or turning someone away making them feel unwanted, undeserving, undesirable, and definitely unloved. Rejection seems so simple, and by definition or concept it is. However, it is much deeper. As stated earlier, it produces after its own kind. As a man, being rejected is like someone stabbing you, and then throwing rubbing alcohol, or salt on the wounds.

It causes you to find other outlets to numb the pain: some

through multiple partners, some through domestic violence, some cope through alcohol, and drug use. At its peak of self-destruction, some men even try to commit suicide. It is immensely hurtful. It leaves you torn in so many directions. It seems like it's a never-ending cycle. Many have experienced some form of rejection whether it's a loved one, a spouse, your friend, even in ministry by a trusted leader, or those in the church.

This type has severe damaging effects on one's mental, spiritual, and emotional wellbeing. It cripples you, paralyzes you with fear, ultimately causing your destiny to be aborted. Rejection leads to the spirit of abandonment which entails that you feel totally isolated, ignored, or non-existent. You have no purpose, and you wear it like a garment. Why though? Why would someone want to make another feel rejected?

There are several factors that make a person reject someone. Trust. Yes, you know the thing that's hard to gain, but so easy to lose. As a man, being able to trust someone is hard, often sometimes seemingly impossible. Trust is breached by the spirit of offense, and/or betrayal. (That's a whole chapter by itself). Hurt is another avenue. Hurt people hurt people. It's not just a slogan, but it is facts. When you have developed the mindset that nobody loves you, nobody cares, and that what you do doesn't matter no matter how much effort you put into it. During this time, you develop a syndrome, that is encapsulated in a vicious cycle making them feel all the pain, anguish, and hurt that you feel.

Lastly, identity issues. As a man, identity is literally not just the biological makeup of the individual, but the physical, emotional, mental, and spiritual embodiment as well. It tells us who we REALLY are. It tells society who we are, it is what makes a man just that a man. Sometimes though, we develop identity issues to where we may fall short. These issues cause us to hide our true self, we are in a place of confusion about life, some with sexuality, and we live in fear of someone knowing our inadequate nature. We tend to try to be somebody we are not to compensate for the low self-esteem, misplaced affections, and uncertainty as to who we really are. This makes you reject someone, and at the same time be the rejected. I want to personally ask you do you want to be healed from rejection, or will you further allow it to direct, and control your life?

Chapter 4

Depression: Silent But Deadly

Have you ever felt "some kind of way" where you couldn't explain? How about losing a loved one or relationship and you're struggling to get over it. You're still grieving, but it seems like your grief is turning into a graveyard. It is safe to say you are going through a period of depression.

We hear about it, but what is depression and how does it relate to me? Depression is defined as a group of conditions, associated with the elevation, or lowering a person's mood. It comes in many forms like clinical depression (mental health disorder characterized by a consistent depressed mood), or loss of interest in activities, causing one's life to be impaired, or paralyzed), persistent depressive disorder, (a mild, but long term form of depression), bipolar disorder, (a disorder associated with episodes of mood swings ranging from depressive lows to manic highs), and lastly bipolar II disorder (a type of disorder characterized by depressive, and hypomanic episodes).

It's often said that depression is like hypertension as it is a silent killer. It is normally characterized by overall sadness, mood changes, lethargy, reduced, or no appetite. On the flip side, men are more irritable, angrier, and engage in risky dangerous behaviors. Men tend to isolate themselves working extra hours, or just staying "low key." Ironically what makes it so dangerous is because you will look for the signs, and many times, it's asymptomatic (having no symptoms). So many men are hurting inside, but can't properly articulate their feelings. Life has taken a toll with so many pressures of being a man.

It is not easy balancing family life, employment and trying to be everything to everyone. Many times, our loved ones enjoy our presence while we suffer in silence. We've been taught to conceal our inner struggles, even when we're hurting the most. Jeremiah 1:18 tells us, "I have made you strong like a fortified city, an iron pillar, and a bronze wall to stand against the whole land…" In other words, it's us against the world. We were created for strength, stamina, and sufficiency, but the truth is we are human, and many times, our weakness is presented as strength. Our sadness is wrapped up in a false smile.

These are just a few reasons why depression is so deadly, and uncompromising. Can you think of one life event that left you at a loss for words? Have you ever been in a place where you couldn't say a word, but your emotions spoke volumes? How did you feel when lost that job that you were employed at for many years? Were you angry? Worried? Did you feel like you couldn't breathe. I'm sure you fell into a low place, where you didn't want to be bothered. You felt hopeless, and helpless. You even got to the place of being angry with God. Yes you, my friend, experienced depression. My final thoughts to you are: do you love yourself to finally admit that you really need help? Are you just having a bad day, or is there a deeper issue beyond the surface? It's okay to admit you're not ok.

Chapter 5

Identity Crisis: Who Am I?

One of the important things in life is knowing who you are. This includes knowing your values, morals, standards, and overall make up that makes you stand out as a person. Yes, I'm talking about your identity. Who am I? Identity gives us the right to belong. Identity gives us favor, and credibility with others. Identity can also be relative according to perspective. Jesus asked a question in Matthew 16:13 regarding His divine identity in their perspective. He asked, "Who do men say that I am"?

Verse 14, there are several responses of identity given such as, "Some say, you are John the Baptist, some Elias, others Jeremias, or one of the prophets." Every man, every living thing has characteristics that specifically mark them, letting others know who they are. A man that walks in confidence, and is sure of his stance in life gains access, and privilege to certain doors that otherwise may not be open. Identity is multi-faceted as it encompasses several areas including physical (what you look like), biological (your DNA and genetic makeup), social (culture, religion, and even how people label you), and lastly spiritual (who you are in God, and your relation to the world through Him).

It is expected as one travel through life, that we know who you are. It is ironic, that a lot of times our identity is not realized until adulthood. Too many, it seems it's never realized. Our identity as a man starts in childhood. We are taught how to be a man by our fathers, or other male figures. We are taught the do's, and dont's of life. We are taught to be self-sufficient, how to be provide, and how to love. Seems simple, but how can I really love when I was never shown it.

You may feel you have never experienced the love from your dad which negatively impacted you. You spent a lot of time in your life trying to 'figure it out', Or even crazier, you had both of your parents, but you still were lost, lonely, and lifeless. So many men, miss the precious moments of their identity being cultivated, and developed. Some men develop an identity that truly is not theirs. They take on what they feel is accepted in other's eyesight. Some had their identity taken from them because of rape, molestation, abuse, confusion, or peer influence. Some even had their identity given to them without a choice. You were told this is who you are like it, or not. This is often attributed to parents' trauma or hard life being deflected on the child.

A child, seeks to imitate or find acceptance, but did not find what he was looking for. As a result, he grew from a boy into the man that was hardened, or confused. He never really had the chance to live out his life, but rather live through the eyes or expectations of someone else. One was expected to act in a certain way, dress a certain way, have a particular profession, even treat family a certain way causing them to directly be affected, often suffering. It was presented one way by the parents, but it was perceived another way.

As a father, we must be careful not to repeat a negative cycle that was impressed upon us. We must be careful, that our ideals and standards don't cause resentment and hatred amongst our children. It is important that we allow our identity to be properly developed, not forced. This is accomplished through life experiences. Through trial and error. Through impartation, support, and love.

Lastly, we must see ourselves the way God sees us. Ultimately, that is where our purest form of identity comes from. We must see ourselves as a success, and not as a failure. We must see ourselves healed, and not broken, winning, and never defeated. We must adapt and live out the decree of Psalms 139:14 "I will praise you because I am fearfully, and wonderfully made". We must live in truth and be who God has called us to be. My question to you, do you really know who you are?

Chapter 6

Abandonment: Dropped, Damaged, Devastated

We see it all the time on shows, hear it in the media, or have heard stories through others about abandonment. To some it seems slightly relatable, to another we can only empathize with the individual, or parties involved. It is often said that a person will never really know how another feels, or how they are affected until it happens to them.

The topic of abandonment can be hard to articulate, difficult to unpack, and seemingly impossible to truly understand the WHY? Why would a person want to abandon someone they say they love? Why would you establish trust, and relationship with a person, then break their heart? Why won't the person who abandoned the other take accountability for their actions? While they became absent, your lifelong pain remained very present.

These questions need answers. As men, we seek closure, and the power to move on. When we begin to speak of abandonment, we understand that it's not just a topic, but it is a spirit that has grown two legs, and has walked in and out of your life, as many have done. To really understand abandonment, you must understand the definition. How is it defined? Abandonment is the state, or action of leaving someone permanently, often when they need you the most for care, protection, or support. It's a form of neglect, carelessness, irresponsibility, and total disregard for the individual's feelings.

During the course, and onset of abandonment, you literally feel these three things: being dropped (the act of abandonment), you are damaged (having the physical/spiritual trauma attached to you), and you become devastated (the mental, and emotional response to the damage/trauma). Remember with any action, there is a response that follows consequently. Even deeper, there are 5 stages of abandonment, that individuals go through. We are talking about SWIRL, not the ice cream flavor, but the acronym that represents the process of healing from the trauma associated with it. Please note that you may experience them differently, and not necessarily in the order of the above acronym.

Let's take a closer look at the first stage, which is SHATTERING. This is the initial shock, and devastation of being abandoned. You know when your whole world crumbles, your left speechless, hurt, can't breathe, and you're in pain. The initial onset honestly hurts the most. to most people, IT COMES WITHOUT WARNING. You were not expecting it. You saw no signs of trouble in paradise, you never thought it would be you.

This stage is one where you can't measure time. Each person is different. It can last from a few minutes, few days, to a few months, and some even push a few years. Again, it's all according to the person, level of impact they experience.

The second stage is WITHDRAWAL. This is where the grim, painful reality of abandonment starts to set in. As depression becomes apparent, you begin to withdraw away from others, experience self-doubt, and craves insatiably attention, and will do whatever is needed to get it. You know how it is, when you withdraw, you start pulling yourself back, to get away, or avoid the situation at hand. It's a case of situational irony, or an oxymoron because as you are withdrawing (pulling away), you are yet being drawn in deeper (pulling towards).

The third stage is INTERNALIZATION. You blame yourself for why it happened. You are trying to make sense of the situation while believing it did not happen, and trying to reason with yourself as well. At this stage you are very vulnerable while feeling inadequate.

Let's move on to stage four which is RAGE/ANGER. In this stage, these emotions are directed at the person who abandoned them, or at the victim. This is where the idea of revenge, (I will make them feel how they made me feel), and self-inflicted harm usually takes place. This is where toxic behaviors really begin to come to the forefront. This is also the stage where your pain pushes you to the place of healing, getting yourself together, and reclaiming the power that was lost.

Last, but not least, we arrive at stage five, which is LIFTING/ACCEPTANCE. This is the stage where clarity, and being ok with the loss takes place. This is where you are healed, and now you can have, and sustain healthy relationships. This is the stage where restoration, and renewal take place. You can trust. You have peace. You are one with yourself, and your heart, and emotions are in equilibrium. Now, as stated earlier, abandonment is not just a topic, or a feeling, but it is a spirit.

Let's take a closer look. The spirit of abandonment or the orphan spirit is spiritual oppression, and mental distress resulting from feelings of being forsaken by God or people. People, men especially, develop this spirit as of result of being dropped, or thrown away by people that we trusted most. Can you remember a time when everything was going well? There were no worries, no concerns. The person, or the people you were in relationship with or covenant with were there for you. All of a sudden, the phone calls stopped, the texts stopped, and they didn't come around anymore. You couldn't understand why. You were the personal ATM for everyone's financial problems. They were there as long as you had means to help. Your hands stayed open, and your pockets are becoming empty, but you did it in the name of God, and your obligation to loyalty.

Some of you I'm sure can remember how you sacrificed for others, put yourself last, and you when your resources dried up so did the communication. It seriously hurt. Even as an adolescent, you remember your dad leaving you, having limited contact with him, and in some cases, he never came around. All you wanted was to be loved. All you wanted was him to be proud of you. All you wanted was for him to be there when you needed him. You didn't want STUFF, you wanted SECURITY. This is the same thing with your mom. You have a constant desire to be loved, not being condemned for mistakes you made, or feeling like you belong.

Please know, many times abandonment is not just a physical state, but it's also a state of PERCEPTION. The spirit abandonment will cause you to believe that everyone who is around you will eventually hurt you. Sooner than later, they will leave like the rest did. You become attracted to the dysfunction, and develop a victim mentality rather than one who walks in victory. You live in defeat, and below standards because you feel you're never good enough.

The spirit of abandonment affects your relationships with others because through it, trust is usually nonexistent, or you trust in hopes that they will stay around. It's also causes you to beg for people to stay in your life. You will do whatever you think makes them happy in hopes they will stay. The spirit of abandonment will cause you to try to find fault in others because of indwelling insecurities. Lastly, it will cause you to become jealous of others who seem to have it all together. It is a perpetual cycle that breeds and feeds after its own kind. I want to leave you with this question: How long will you let abandonment cripple your life?

Chapter 7

Unforgiveness: The Corrosive Cancerous Cycle

Have you ever looked at somebody, and bad feelings came up? When you think about something that happened, and the person involved: Do you find yourself uneasy? Bothered? Angy? You, my friend, are experiencing the symptoms, and effects of unforgiveness. This is something one struggles with, often daily because it feels better to be petty than to be pleasant.

Naturally, we want and we like the satisfaction of making someone feel the sting of our words, and pain from our words or hands, by getting them told, or making them feel lesser. Instant gratification, right? While this is pleasing, on the flip side it is also poisonous to your life. Unfortunately, unforgiveness is one that feels good. We think we have let something go, but in actuality it's not DEAD, but it is simply DORMANT, and DELIVERANCE is needed. Now, that I have your attention, what is unforgiveness?

It is the refusal to let go of resentment, and anger towards someone who has done you wrong. You're bitter, revengeful, and unwilling to be the bigger person by forgiving.

It is a deep emotional, and mental state that shows up as a significant burden adversely affecting one's thoughts, emotions, and behaviors. It can get worse over a period of time. In simpler terms, you won't let stuff go. You're harboring things in your heart. You allow circumstances, and things of the past to fester, until it overtakes you and your polluted.

It is similar to cancer that is spreading fast. Unforgiveness is fueled by the spirit of offense which is the mindset of holding onto negativity, anger, and bitterness it leads to the unwillingness to forgive. It is a constant sense of being the victim, and misinterpreting someone's words or actions. It is a mental and emotional state rooted in pride.

This is a recipe that hinders spiritual growth, trust, and relationships. You might be curious as to know why unforgiveness is similar to cancer or like cancer, it is a disease that causes significant damage. It can manifest as a destructive internal state that often leads to emotional strain or turmoil such as: anger, depression, bitterness, resentment, hate, and even cause physical harm (stress, cancer, strokes, heart attacks, stomach issues etc). It spreads and can damage your entire body.

When you hold onto unforgiveness, you develop negative thoughts, distorted views, and perceptions, chronic explosive anger, often mirroring cancer. There are four key characteristics of unforgiveness that one can struggle with. First is resentment, and bitterness. What do I mean? It's the persistent, uncompromising feeling of indignation (that is anger caused by something you feel wasn't right). Secondly, is demand for punishment/payback. You desire to hurt the one who hurt you, or you want an apology that you feel you deserve. Often times though, the apology that is desired will never happen, so the cycle continues. Third, there is the inability to release the one who offended you. As a man, our level of stubbornness, pride, and overall ego will not allow clearance to let them go because of perception, and stance. Lastly, there is emotional distress.

Unforgiveness makes a toxic environment leading to more negative emotions festering then manifesting. My friend, my brother, it's time to do a self-evaluation. Are you holding something against someone? Yes, I know you say, "I'm fine", "I let it go", "it's water under the bridge", but is that really the case? What is triggering you to act the way you do? Can you honestly say if you see that person, or you go to that familiar place, you're unbothered? We often can't discern the difference between what's dormant, or dead because we are blinded to the truth. Some know the truth but feel it's safer to ignore it rather than to address it, and get the help that's needed.

My friend, allow me to speak to your heart, perhaps you're struggling with forgiving a family member, or maybe your spouse, what about your accuser? What about the one who tried to take your manhood? As long as you hold it in, you hold yourself back. You become a prisoner, captive to your own emotions. Free yourself. Let go, and forgive.

Chapter 8

Betrayal: Charged With Attempted Murder

First 48, Law & Order, NCIS, and the Wire. What do all these shows have in common? They all deal with crime, the victims that are targeted, and ultimately hurt. Why is that relevant? Betrayal deals with all three of these same factors. In one's perspective It is a crime (it causes physical or psychological harm), a victim is targeted (normally involves two or more parties where the betrayed was already sought out, or talked about with the enemy), and the course of action left them hurt and broken.

When you think of betrayal what truly comes to mind? Is it someone you trusted with everything? You shared your deepest darkest secrets, your hearts concerns, and they turned on you. Could it be the person you told your dreams to, or shared your vision, and aspirations in life, and they tried to sabotage you? What about family members you confided in, and they assassinated your character.

Lastly, what about in ministry? You gave, and went far beyond to make sure the needs of the ministry were taken care of, and it wasn't appreciated. Or what about when God elevated you, to do the work He has assigned to your hands? Your friends turned foe because of jealousy. They turned against you, and caused others to turn against you as well.

Betrayal is one of the most hurtful, painful situations, or positions a person can be in. It literally feels like you're drowning, or you are being repeatedly stabbed in the back after giving your all to a person. It's hard to explain, but being stabbed in the back by someone you love feels like a new level of hurt, and disrespect. Like abandonment, many times it comes without warning. This is why it leaves you in such a place of disbelief, or shock. So many questions arise like how did this happen? What did I do wrong? I thought we were solid? Let's go a little deeper on this subject.

To understand betrayal, we have to define it. How is it defined? One definition is to be led astray. (Seduce). Another definition is to deliver to your enemy by treachery (which is the violation of allegiance or disloyalty). Many have experienced both. We have been seduced, or lead astray into thinking that the ones we counted on were solid, had a bond that was unbreakable, but something changed. Perhaps, it was the power of influence someone had over the one that betrayed you. Most of us have had an encounter with being handed over to our enemies.

This is not, really, just physical, but also mental,

spiritual, and emotional. When you are betrayed one major sign of how you are affected is by your response. Men, respond to betrayal like anyone else through intense (and I mean intense) emotional, and psychological reactions like anger, confusion, self-esteem issues, and trust is definitely shattered. Men also at times may experience certain emotions like shame, rejection, and guilt. Betrayal can severely damage a man's viewpoint on himself. We may feel emasculated, rejected, or feel like we're not good enough. At times, we will blame ourselves for what happened.

Have you ever found yourself after the betrayed blaming yourself for what happened? The more you internalized, reasoned, and thought about it the worse it got. It gets a little deeper. Betrayal is bad within itself, but it triggers other conditions to arise. When triggered, after such a traumatic event, now you don't trust, you don't feel safe, and you can develop mental instabilities that will cause you to be dysfunctional. Your relationships suffer because you don't know if it will happen again. Trust is shattered immensely, and very hard to get back. For men, it increases our level of pride (which God hates), it causes walls to be built, to protect our broken heart.

As you read this chapter, take a look inside yourself. Who are you hurting because you have been betrayed by someone? You must understand that it doesn't just affect you, but the ones closest to you. The ones connected to you. One thing is for certain, you can only conceal the hurt for so long, and then it begins to bleed out of the wound that was created. It comes out when you speak, how you preach, through your actions, and interactions. It shapes your perspectives, thought processes, and even how you serve God and people. Hurt people hurt people as said before. Think about it. Don't you owe it to yourself to no longer be a victim? Even though, the attack was meant to kill you, you yet have a reason to live. You have purpose to pursue, and greatness to achieve.

Chapter 9

Pride: Chest Out, Heart Broken, Chest Out

Have you ever met someone that was too arrogant, or cocky for their own good? You couldn't tell them anything. They find a way to dispute, or contend with you to prove a point every time. Normally you can tell a person that has pride based on the use of the letter "I". Everything is about them. You, my friend, have experienced someone operating in the spirit of pride. This is one of seven things God hates according to Proverbs 6. It is referred to as a "proud look". That's just it. It's a look. A shell that hides the real you inside.

What exactly is the spirit of pride? How do we define it as a subject? It is defined as spiritual pride characterized by excessive self-focus (being stuck on ones yourself), arrogance, a sense of superiority (can't be touched, one feels they are above anyone or anything), and the belief that you can make it by yourself, you don't need any help from anyone including God Himself. It manifests as a resistance to prayer, wisdom, or prophecy. Pride will make you have a harsh demeanor, judge others unfairly, condemn, and not show grace, or mercy to those who need it. At the end it leads to a major downfall. The Bible in Proverbs 16:18-19 declares, "Pride goeth before destruction, and a haughty spirit before a fall".

There is definitely a line between confident & cocky. One is exalting God; the other is exalting self. There are characteristics, or symptoms of the spirit of pride. Firstly, there is EXCESSIVE SELF-FOCUS, and DEPENDANCE. This entails the person is self-centered, selfish, and deceived that they are capable of handling things on their own.

Secondly, there is SPIRITUAL SUPERIORITY, and ARROGANCE. This spirit makes a person feel spiritually, and physically superior to others. They believe they have God figured out. It is believed that you have control, and at its worse state, you are deceived into thinking you're equal to God, and look at others as your servants.

Thirdly, the spirit of pride makes one RESISTANT TO GOD'S INTERVENTION. Pride will make you not pray and seek wise council. It will not allow you to seek the will of God in your life. It will make you too ashamed to ask for help. You would rather suffer, than to appear needy, and get assistance.

Next, pride will make you have a CRITICAL and CONDEMNATORY attitude. This will make you forget that you were once something until God saved you. This spirit makes you go against Romans 3:23 which declares, "For all have sinned, and fallen short of the glory of God". It causes you to find fault in others, and you point out their flaws, while neglecting your own.

Lastly, pride will KEEP YOU FROM ADMITTING YOU WERE WRONG. In other words, it's your way or no way. You won't apologize because you are standing ten toes down on your view that you are right. There is no compromise. There is no grey area. This is why it's so dangerous, this spirit can be operating in you, and you don't know it. It tends to cloak itself, mask itself, or adapt to its surroundings. Many times, before a person realizes that this spirit is in operation, they have already been blinded or deceived, and it has pushed them to the point where damage has been done. It's like you're too prideful, to even see that you have pride.

As men, it is really dangerous for us because many times we operate in this spirit daily, and it's normal. A lot of it started when we were younger, our parents, or other trusted voices telling us, "if you don't have it, don't ask". It's at that moment that the seed was planted. We let it grow, until it became a monster. Originally, pride started with Satan, before the fall of humanity. Then it happened in the Garden of Eden in Genesis. Why is pride such a struggle amongst men? For many of us we can't really tell how we feel. We don't want to look weak, or not appear in control of certain affairs in our lives. We are taught that only the strong survive. We face bouts of pride competing with others.

We have a tendency to be better than the next man. These are all facts indeed, but I want you to really begin to think about what happened in your life that made you prideful. As we go through life, and experience different things, it can cause our hearts to be hardened, even broken because of hurt, pain, grief, disappointment, and discouragement.

You develop the mindset that "I will never let this happen again", so you develop an alter ego, a pseudo human that on the outside you are strong and resilient, on the inside your heart is broken into pieces. You want to protect it, so you build a wall. Nothing gets in, nothing gets out. This wall is similar to the rib cage, and the sternum that is set in place to protect the heart from physical trauma. The wall is now there that while you are healing (or so you think), it's actually causing more trauma, and greater damage.

You, my friend may ask the question why can't I receive love? The answer is, you operate from a guarded place. Your level of pride won't let you explore and try again. You miss many opportunities of growth, and experiences of life because you are afraid. Pride makes you comfortable, and fearful of the unknown. It is a spirit that must be broken, cast out, and repented of. It is one as said earlier that made Lucifer feel as if he is equal to God, and he could not be touched which led him to fall. Look deep inside yourself and ask yourself "do I exhibit any of these signs"? "Am I blind to my own shortcomings"?

Destroy pride before it destroys you.

Scriptures

Psalm 119:105

"Thy Word is a lamp unto my feet, and a light unto my path"
As you make this journey to healing, wholeness, redemption, and recovery, here are some scriptures that will help, and encourage you to keep going and keep growing.

Addiction:

Proverbs 25:28
"A man without self-control is like a city broken into, and left without walls"

2 Timothy 1:7
"For God has not given us the spirit of fear, but power, love, and a sound mind"

Titus 2:11-12
"For the grace of God has appeared, bringing salvation for all people, training us to renounce ungodliness, and worldly passions, and to live self-controlled, upright, and Godly lives in the present age"

1 Corinthians 10:13
"No temptation has overtaken you that is not common to man. God is faithful, and He will not let you be tempted beyond your ability, but with the temptation He will also provide the way of escape, that you may be able to endure it."

Abuse

Isaiah 40:29-31
"He gives power to the weak, and to those who have no might He increases strength. They that wait upon the Lord shall renew their strength. They shall mount up on wings like eagles, they run and not be weary, they shall walk and not faint "

Matthew 11:28
" Come to ME all who labour, and are heavy laden, and I will give you rest"

Psalm 9:9
"The Lord is a stronghold for the oppressed, a stronghold in the time of trouble"

Rejection

Luke 10:16
"The one who hears you, hears ME, the one who rejects you rejects ME, and the one who rejects ME, rejects the One who sent ME"

Jeremiah 30:17
"For I will restore health unto you, and your wounds will I heal, declares the Lord because they called you an outcast"

Isaiah 43:4
"Because you are precious in my eyes, honored, and I love you, I give men in return for you, and give people for your life"

Depression

Isaiah 41:10
"Fear not, for I am with you: be not dismayed for I am your God. I will strengthen you, I will help you, I will uphold you with my righteous hand."

Psalm 30:5
"For His anger is for a moment, and His favor is for life. Weeping may endure for a night, but joy comes in the morning."

Psalm 3:3
"But thou oh Lord, are a shield for me, my glory , the lifter of my head."

Identity Crisis

Ephesians 2:10
"For we are his workmanship, created in Christ Jesus, for good works beforehand, that we should walk in them."

1 Peter 2:9
"But ye are a chosen generation, a royal priesthood, an holy nation, a peculiar people; that ye should shew forth the praises of him who hath called you out of darkness into his marvellous light:"

2 Corinthians 5:17
"Therefore, if any man be in Christ, he is a new creature: old things are passed away; behold, all things are become new."

Abandonment

Psalm 68:5
"God in His holy dwelling is a father of the fatherless and a champion of widows."

Psalm 27:10
" Even if my mother, and father forsake me, the Lord will hold me close"

Matthew 28:20
"Surely I am with you always, to the very end of the age."

Unforgiveness

Matthew 7:14
"For if you forgive other people when they sin against you, your heavenly Father will also forgive you."

Ephesians 4:31
" Get rid of all bitterness, rage and anger, brawling and slander, along with every form of malice."

Mark 11:25
" And when you stand praying, if you hold anything against anyone, forgive them, so that your Father in heaven may forgive you your sins."

Betrayal

Psalm 109:4
"In return for my friendship they accuse me, but I am a man of prayer."

Proverbs 19:5
"A false witness will not go unpunished, and one who utters lies will not escape."

Psalm 41:9
"Even my friend in whom I trusted, one who ate my bread, has raised his heel against me."

Pride

James 4:6
" But He gives greater grace. Therefore, He says: God resists the proud, but gives grace to the humble."

Proverbs 11:2
"When pride comes, disgrace follows, but with humility comes wisdom."

Romans 12:3
" For by the grace given to me, I tell everyone among you not to think of himself more highly than he should think. Instead, think sensibly, as God has distributed a measure of faith to each one."

What are your Triggers?

The word (trigger) describes situations, words, or experiences that stir up emotional mental reactions, painful memories, past trauma or physical reactions. A trigger can be anything external or internal, which can lead a person toward sin or fear or provokes reactions that can pull a person away from peace, obedience, and trust in God.

A trigger can also be considered a stumbling block that can cause a person to fall back into sin. Romans 14:13 states, "Make up your mind not to put any stumbling block or obstacle in the way of a brother or sister."

There are times where one experiences a memory that leads to old wounds and reminds them of their hurtful and painful past. Israel was often "triggered" back into fear or rebellion when reminded of past hardships. Exodus 16:3 "when hungry, the people remembered Egypt and complained instead of trusting God.

One can be healed from their trigger issues once they have first acknowledged the issue and then the renewing of the mind will take place. The word of God has called us to be transformed by the renewing of our mind.

As the word states in Proverbs 15:1 "A gentle answer turns away wrath, but a harsh word stirs up anger." We have to overcome our triggers with God's word. The great part about it is we are not powerless and no longer have to live in bondage to our triggers. We are overcomers and victorious. Start today we will take our thoughts captive and make it obedient to God.

Triggers are real. What are your triggers? When we understand triggers, they no longer have to control us. Instead, they can become opportunities for growth, healing, and victory in Christ.

As you continue to read below there is a list of questions that will help you understand your triggers. Look at this a kickstart to your healing. As you answer the questions, be honest with yourself so nothing is overlooked or missed.

Triggers Questionnaire

Purpose: This tool helps you become more aware of the situations, people, thoughts, and environments that activate strong emotions or behaviors.

Section 1: Awareness of Emotional Triggers
Instructions: Rate each item from 1 (Never) to 5 (Always)

1. I notice myself feeling defensive when criticized.
2. I get anxious in crowded or noisy environments.
3. I feel anger rising when I perceive unfair treatment.
4. I feel shame or embarrassment when I make mistakes.
5. I experience sadness when I feel ignored or left out.
6. I feel overwhelmed when too many demands are placed on me.
7. I get irritated when plans don't go as expected.

Section 2: Awareness of Behavioral Triggers
Instructions: Rate each item from 1 (Never) to 5 (Always)

8. I reach for food, substances, or distractions when stressed.
9. I procrastinate when I feel pressured or overwhelmed.
10. I shut down or withdraw when conflicts arise.
11. I lash out verbally when I feel disrespected.
12. I avoid tasks or people that bring up uncomfortable feelings.
13. I overcommit to things when I'm afraid of disappointing others.
14. I act impulsively when I feel excited or restless.

Section 3: Situational Triggers
Check all that apply to you:

☐ Being criticized

☐ Feeling excluded

☐ Uncertainty about the future

☐ Authority figures

☐ Conflict with loved ones

☐ Deadlines or time pressure

☐ Crowds or noise

☐ Financial stress

☐ Physical discomfort (tired, hungry, sick)

☐ Others: _____

Section 4: Reflection Questions (Open-Ended)
15. Think of the last time you felt a strong emotional reaction. What was the situation?
16. What emotions did you notice first? (e.g., anger, sadness, anxiety, guilt)
17. How did you respond behaviorally? (e.g., lash out, shut down, overeat, avoid)
18. Did the reaction feel automatic or intentional?
19. Looking back, what might have been the trigger?
20. What helps you calm down or regain control when you're triggered?

Section 5: Coping & Growth
21. Which triggers feel the most frequent for you?
22. Which triggers cause the strongest reactions?
23. What coping strategies do you already use that work?
24. What new strategies would you like to try?

Next Step: After completing, look for patterns (e.g., criticism, rejection, uncertainty) and link them to your go-to behaviors. That's where awareness can lead to change.

SWIRL Quiz: The Five Stages of Abandonment

This quiz is designed to help you identify which stage of abandonment you may be experiencing. For each statement, rate yourself from 1 (Not true for me) to 5 (Very true for me).

S – Shattering
___I feel like my world has completely fallen apart.
___I struggle to make sense of what just happened.
___I feel numb or in shock about the loss.

W – Withdrawal
___I have a deep craving for the person or situation I lost.
___I feel restless, anxious, or emotionally dependent.
___I want to "fix" things, even if it means ignoring my own needs.

I – Internalizing
___I blame myself for what happened.
___I feel unworthy of love or acceptance.
___I constantly replay events in my mind, wondering what I did wrong.

R – Rage
___I feel angry about being left, betrayed, or ignored.
___I find myself resenting the person or situation.
___I feel bursts of frustration that are hard to control.

L – Lifting
___I am beginning to accept what happened.
___I notice glimpses of hope for the future.
___I am reconnecting with myself and rebuilding my life.

Scoring
- Add up the scores in each section (S, W, I, R, L).
- The highest total suggests your current stage in the abandonment cycle.

Note: People may move back and forth between stages. This quiz is not a diagnosis but a tool for self-awareness and healing.

Resources for Men's Wellbeing

Man Therapy
www.mantherapy.org

Man's Resource Center of West Michigan
www.menscenter.org
Phone: (616) 456-1178

Alcoholic Anonymous
www.aa.org

SAMHSA (Subtance Abuse and Mental Health Services Administration)
www.samhsa.gov
1-800-662-HELP (4357)
Text 435748

988 Suicide and Crisis Lifeline
www.988lifeline.org
Dial 988 or text 988

Face It Foundation
www.faceitfoundation.org
Phone: (651)-200-4297
Email: info@faceitfoundation.org

Black Men Heal
www.blackmanheal.org
Email: info@blackmenheal.org

About the Author

Worshipper, Family Man, Trailblazer, Entrepreneur, Songwriter, Musician, Apostolic/Prophetic Voice, Pastor, and now Author. This is Dr. David W. Bland. God's Chosen for such a time as this. He is a true survivor, and a man of many gifts for the glory of God. He is a Kingdom builder, a lover of God's people, and a friend to many.

www.ingramcontent.com/pod-product-compliance
Lightning Source LLC
Chambersburg PA
CBHW071231160426
43196CB00012B/2478